WORD HAS IT
Poems

WORD HAS IT

Poems

Ruth Danon

Nirala

Nirala Publications
4637/20, Unit no 310, Third Floor,
Hari Sadan,, Ansari Road
Daryaganj, New Delhi-110002
niralabooks@yahoo.co.in
www.niralapublications.com

_____

First Edition 2018

_____

ISBN 81-8250-097-4

_____

Copyright©Ruth Danon

_____

Cover Art: Gary Buckendorf

_____

Book Layout: Tanmay Sardar

_____

Printed at
Chaman Offset Press
New Delhi-2

For
Ann Beattie

Contents

Acknowledgments

I am grateful to the editors who published my work, sometimes in slightly different form or with different titles.

"Habitual," *The Five-Two*

"An Act of Faith in a Simple Time," "Americana," "Season of Uneasy," *Resist Much, Obey Little* (anthology)

"Approach," "The Joke," *The Florida Review*

"Floridian," *Isthmus*

"Habitation," (section 11), *NOON: The Journal of the Short Poem*

"Habitation," (entire text) forthcoming, *Tupelo Quarterly*

"Birding," *Mead: The Journal of Literature and Libation*

"Augury," *Augury Books*

I appreciate so deeply the many who have helped me and cheered me along as this book came into being. They are listed below, in alphabetical order.

Heide Arbitter, David Austell, Ann Beattie Martine Bellen, Vicky Bijur, William Burns, Neil Blackadder, Kathleen Caprario, Michael Coppola, Martha Danon, Kristina Marie Darling, Sally Dawidoff, Jennifer Egan, Anita Feldman, Elisabeth Frost, Lisa Fugard, Michael Golder, Gail Goldsmith, David Groff, Ken Hart, Linda Herrick, Amy Hoffman, Amy Holman, Melissa Hotchkiss, Kathleen Hulley, Christine Kelly, Susan Kinsey, April Krassner, Robert Lapiner, Carl Lebowitz, Jeffrey Levine, Andrew Levy, Kristin Lovejoy, David Lichtenstein, Stephen

Massimilla, Hermine Meinhard, Ken Northington, Clinton Davidson Murphy, Suzanne Parker, Lincoln Perry, David Rich, Paulette Myers-Rich, Natania Rosenfeld, David Rosenstock, Phyllis Rosser, Elaine Sexton, Rosalind ,Solomon, Roberta Stone, Julia Strayer, Elizabeth Tippens .Chase Twichell, Rob Wilson, and Yael Yisraeli

Outside and beyond the alphabetical I must thank, particularly:

Yuyutsu Ram Dass Sharma, who made this book possible. First, he recognized me and my work; then he asked me to write the book; then he shepherded it through Nirala. He has been a kind support throughout this process. I am grateful beyond words.

Gary Buckendorf, my husband and life partner, who gave me permission to use his beautiful drawing on the cover of this book.

I also thank Nirala Press for accepting a book by a relatively unknown American writer, attending to it with care and attention, and for making the process a pleasure.

WORD HAS IT
Poems

I
RUMOR, MURMUR

The essence is hidden from us. . .

(Wittgenstein, Philosophical Investigations)

Interruption

I attempt travel. I fail, missing the train,
or the boat, so to speak. These accidents
prove lucky, in some strange way, forcing
me into a few quiet moments, quiet enough
to, for example, read a book and laugh out
loud, thus breaking the silence and the mood
that can only be described as foreboding.
Change happens. Another train arrives, late.

I climb aboard.

word was
        on the street
and we needed
to know
that much

the word was
        not the one
we wanted
        no, not at all

Habitual

In the circle of light that interrupts the early dark she pursues
foreign mysteries. Do not take this as metaphor. Rather, she,
the writer, has become obsessed, it's fair to say, with mystery
novels written by people she doesn't know set in places she's
never seen. The crimes are appalling – serial murder pursued
as performance art. Spike-loaded apples, aberrant snowmen,
and so on. Clues are heavy on archetype. Some readers will
recognize the allusions. It doesn't matter, though; the point
is clear enough. Murders in books are acts of imagination
but after a while the mysteries become quotidian. The writer
acquires mysteries with increasing frequency, first delaying the
purchase to avoid guilt, then acquiring a mystery almost ever
day because the pleasure is too intense to refuse. She learns
that serial murderers begin to leave less and less time between
crimes because the kick doesn't last. The writer understands
this. The body gone, there is only language. Serial murderers
leave notes, write in code. They grow increasingly impatient.
They hate the dark. They want to be found.

An Act of Faith in a Simple Time

Now, late in the season, I am, inexplicably,
obsessed with spies. Anyone could turn up
with a secret. Anyone could be someone else.
It's why I sit outside at this cafe, twirling
the stem of a wine glass, pretending to
drink pinot noir. Alert to the sudden
motion in the street, I raise my eyes. Now
the firemen drift slowly down the avenue
carrying hatchets, bearing their own
names across their backs. Or so they say.
Who's to say they haven't switched coats?
Who's to say there's a fire?

word spills the beans
all over
    the circus floor

pity the ringmaster
horse rider, pity
too, the tiny
cannon, the pure clown

Approach

Close on to the longest night of the year,
moon just past full. Nothing to declare, I walk
through customs, papers in one hand, luggage
in the other. Gatekeepers nod. Gatekeepers
never know what I carry, what I leave
behind: revelation; rival gangs of angels;
oranges and lemons; crimson amaranth:
time before trouble.

Entry

Long journey between strange hills:

difficult to tell the difference between
the stopping and starting.

The Future

A tiny historical breeze was blowing in
and all around the people were yelling
"herding cats, herding cats." As far as I
could tell, no herds and no cats.
Little did I know times were changing;
days tightening up, darker and colder and
anger coming into the station, noisy, like
an empty train late at night. Edgy, now, I
wait, fists closed tight, the yelling over.
Then, into the station runs one striped
cat, lost and small, chasing a tail.

word flies all over town
     in many quarters
          huddle and nod
in many quarters
          puzzle and frown
who knew word
     could travel so far
     so fast in so little time?

Compulsion and Sorrow

I tell one story and then another story and always it's the
same story about the lost bees. They swarmed and left.

What was broken remains broken:
tree limbs after the storm strewn all over the yard.

That was something that happened so I count other things:
socks,stones, feathers on the ground, a basket of eggs.

How many times did I fill a glass of water and put it beside
me at night?
And how many times was it still full in the morning?

I dream of presence. I dream this often. How often?
Ten times? Twenty? And then I forget.

I count again. Counting on it again.
Brushing my long hair every morning.

I tell one story, then another, and it is always the same story.

Little Defeats

Adept at ruin, I shake out the white flag,
name no alternative, hold

out one hand, withhold the other. When it's rain
all bets are off. It's water and flood.

No ark in this storm, no parade, no
two by two by two.

word breaks
       at the point
of perfection
feckless,
       wild
with
       so much
wanting

"The Need for Disorder"

After Calvino

Here in this dusk studded city we have methods and tactics.
That is why we specialize in lightly fingered melodies
after the fact. This leads to tentative virtuosity in the morning.

You, player that you are, tell a story about your
tenuous attachment to the word "little" in both word
and deed. Wisteria and floribunda come to mind.

You wanted just this once to be the sort of person who knows
the names of flowers. The green mercy of the garden forgives
you far more than you deserve.

Americana

Surcharge for credit in the city of angels. I was foolish in ways I didn't know possible. The sky streaks and then, later, tiny lights come on in the hills. They call this a basin. It goes on for miles. Can I wash my hands in dust? Can I wash my hands? They call this the golden land and it stretches out beyond relief. Now, no heat in the Millennium Hotel and a lone bug trawling the line of sight. After that, the breaking point.

words
with power
to interrupt sleep
the bad taste
endures
still
the small
papers
slip
into the mouth
one then
one more

Clue

Ghost of a fingernail
     we chewed on once,
then ripped to the quick.
     The pain made us
draw breath. You, then
me, then both of us together.

Floridian

Now, interior heat. Small fire
burning slowly in a small room.
Time was. Oh yes. And is. And
now a going forth, a late birth.
Unseasonable chill in the palms.
Fronds I mean, and also the cold
fingertips that touch them. Lizard
facing down the tree, then up.
I wouldn't hazard its quick turn.

word had a long look
down the avenue and then up
to cirrus streaks in relentless
blue, down then up, down,
then up, up then down, flip
that frame

The Joke

A friend once told me of a woman who plays the harp in the rooms of the dying. It is said that this gives comfort and eases the passage out of this life into whatever there is on what people call the other side.   Music for the far edge of faltering consciousness. It made a pretty story. But it was not clear to me who was most comforted – the dying one, fading out of consciousness, the harp player, or the person telling the story. Consciousness is edgy. On another night a man reads a story about going batshit in Kansas City. The audience thought this was funny, what the writer referred to as high hilarity. That was what he told them he would provide. But of course it wasn't funny. It was terrifying, the extremes of paranoia and delusion closing in on him in a fading, not too clean hotel in the middle of the country. If might have been the end of the world and the end of time. There were no harps.

Voyeur

The angry receptionist stepped away
as light, evidence of that day's breadth,
faded into dark. I could say "theatrical"
but it wasn't really, just a slipping away
and a quiet exit. A few stayed late for
the after party. They'd started whispering
before it began. The book was filled with
names. So much scrawl. So much black
ink. Words are so big.

word is out but
much too late

what can be done?
what to say?

anyway word
has it

true enough
harsh enough

word waits
and waits

word washes
her dirty
little hands
of it

Season of Uneasy

It wasn't exactly a personal matter and certainly had something to do with the times themselves.

We didn't actually know the outcome of random choices, that glass of wine or not, that day in the park when the dogs were fighting by the big tree.

And certainly we had better things to do with our time than hold up traffic.

Don't bet on the outcome. Rein in those dogs.

Wear your red scarf and hat it's windy enough to worry.

Underneath the calm was something else.

"Underneath" is a complicated preposition, inexact in certain ways.

I am my own worst enemy. Maybe.

None of this is political, exactly.

But all of this has to do with power, the lack thereof.

Some of it requires language, the presence of.

The red scarf and hat need to be purchased.

That is a matter of money.

The worry underneath the calm.

The old two- step.

One dances, one doesn't.

One wants to speak.

One doesn't.

word fails
         and fails again
but not better
nor bitter
not this time

this edge is
edgy   time
is, was, only time
this time, though,
words fail

At the arrival of stupefying darkness

let me make up a story, let it be
a good one.

It's true isn't it, true that
you pulled your hat down over your eyes.

I can't see a way out.

You were waiting at the street comer for me, only me,
and I was
slow to recognize the greeting, the calm movement of
one hand.

Not so bad, but bad enough.

I could do something with scarves,
I think,
tie them around my head or around my waist.

A costume suited to your hat.

I'm an accessory after the fact.

It was, after all, a kind of murder, wasn't it?

Clever you.

Clever me.

The Gates

What's left of the past holds me:
arches of ancient cities and the gifts
of patrons and gods. The word "lapis"
comes to mind as well as "fig" and "duty"
- as in that which must be paid

II
EVERY ROOM
IN THE HOUSE

"To be a poet . . . you must
set your house on fire and walk away. "

- Yuyutsu Sharma

Novel

There is, always, in abeyance, a
story to tell, a first event leading
to a second and a second to a third
and all of this taking place in a leafy
setting something like a park with a
fountain splashing in it and people all
around admiring the dogs that come
in many sizes and shapes and colors
such that the impression is given that
no one exists who does not have a dog.

She does not have a dog, I note in margin.
But the possibility gives rise to the
petting of one dog and then another
and the murmuring of phrases so familiar
as to be soothing, as in "good dog," good
dog." Don't you want the story to start?
As in something happening relative to
the people with their dogs and the
fountain splashing and the whole sky
turning blush and the evening coming on.

It's time for an entrance, a person, a
specific person, she, perhaps, wearing
a new dress adorned with that red scarf
artful over her shoulders, and walking
casually over the stones aware that 1) she
is not alone in the park and 2) that someone
or no one is looking at her.

It matters whether one or two is true.
And so, here I am, in a quandary, She
and the possible or impossible other
about to meet or not meet. And if they
meet then many things could happen.
If they don't the same is true.

She might walk on proud in loneliness
towards the river. She might stand
by the water a while, and then return
home, stopping on the way for a coffee
and ice cream in a local parlor, where
prices are way too high, but isn't that
the way it always is with pleasure,
prices can get way too high?

And if they do meet they might have
a conversation, about dogs and their
habits, about the color and texture
of the sky. They might walk slowly
together away from the river to one
apartment or another, hers, or his,
and as he removes her black dress
for the first time, you, dear reader,
start to wonder where the story ends.

Beauty, Where You Find It

Five fingers of each hand pressed flat and wide across the tabletop. This a start to pushing herself into standing with a straight back and a better outlook. There are so many ways of being lonely; she's rehearsing them all, as many as she can name. The pretty scarf, the color of sunset, hangs around her neck. Who thought she could be so burdened? Who thought she would take it on?

Domestic

"Shot of whiskey," she thought, from
nowhere, not because she ever drank
the stuff, but because it seemed the kind
of random association one might have at
the end of a long day. Beauty is what she
wanted to be, but didn't know the first
thing about. "Shot through with light,"
was an expression she liked. Radiance or
the idea of glowing from within seemed
a worthy aspiration. Unruly she was,
actually, and messy, useless papers and
books crashing to the floor, and she too
defeated to pick them up. At least,
capable now of candor when she looked
in the mirror, she saw limit smudging
her eyes. She looked ahead, steady
on her feet, or so she thought.

Habitation

1.

If I inhabit the whole house I will suffer no more sorrow than if I inhabit only a single room. I walk from one to the next through doors and passageways, through what I know and what becomes strange in the moment of passage, liminal and urgent.

2.

And that long breath, that hesitation, was a way of betraying something I hadn't known. For some reason I thought of oysters, closed up in their shells and the hard work of prying them open. I didn't know why I thought of them, except they seemed vulnerable, there in the water they yielded when split in two

3.

What will I carry with me
as I move from room to room?
What will I pick up? What
will I set down
on the quiet ledge of the mantel?

4.

I journey, now, from one room to another,
Call it night habitation, lamps dimmed,
one by one, and the slow turn of the hours.

5.

Something about habitation requires work and frequent acts of attention. In the big body of the refrigerator I place a white bowl filled with some leftover tagine; the rest I place in a plastic container to freeze. It can be said that today I have inhabited different rooms of the refrigerator. Today I learned that in another room, far from here, a poet suggested that rooms open us to glimpses of the soul. Today, so many glimpses, brief, fleeting, and so cold.

6.

Light through my window, light behind my eyes, light playing against shadows on the floor, light illuminating the clock with hands that don't move, my hand brushing the floor, the cracks in the floor opening to time, my hand in a little fist, moving away from the floor, holding on a bit longer before the light fades.

7.

Maggie, big of eye and tail, is looking for an opening.
What she wants is to pry open the lid of the blanket chest I
inherited from my mother. What she wants is what she wants.
The books are in her way. She doesn't care. She wants an
opening. Her paws push and pry. She's all frustration. She
won't give up, until she does.

8.

Nothing more than a first gesture, a sheet folded over to create a perception of calm. The day held its heat and the show of animals went on. A man with a white bird on his shoulder, another with a black cat on his head. Pigeons flock and sparrows hide in the spaces between. Later, inside, the air conditioner hums. The sheets open up.

9.

Sometimes, after I've washed the dishes after a simple late dinner, after the cat has been fed in the hallway, after I sip a cup of tea on the red sofa, after the bath and the quiet time of writing, after turning down the cool sheets on the newly made bed, I feel that every room I inhabit has moved inside me. I curl into sleep and the rooms settle inside me; then, after all that, the rooms murmur desire that I inhabit them again.

10.

The dark is crowding me out. Feet,
can I follow that sliver of light
into the next room?

11.

Message from a room
formerly filled
with light:

Nothing prepared me
for inquisition
or pilgrimage. Not
cold stones, not bare feet.

12.

Standing outside the door, the door
locked, I imagine the inside
and the fire burning. I wait,
I wait for a long time. Then I
put on my pretty leather gloves
and my feathered hat and fly away.

III
DIVINATION

I shall only take notice that all arts were begot by chance and observation and nursed by use and experience, and improved and perfected by reason and study. Thus we are told that physic was invented in a thousand thousand years by a thousand thousand men and so, too, the art of navigation: as, indeed, all other arts have grown by degree from the smallest beginnings.

- Leone Batisti Alberti
The Ten Books of Architecture

Doubt

No reasoning beyond reason
as thirst is only thirst
and a measure of what's been lost
in the madness of heat.
       Someone named
the birds for me and I
could see reason in their names:
The bluebird is, after all,
blue and bears itself before
me in a barren tree.
       If I study
drought long enough
I will see blue veins
under my skin, a track
without oratory, perhaps,
but not without history
       Now parsed
pure, inevitably, my
pursed lips parch.

Birding

So listen, let me confess, I do not live in a world
that lends itself easily to description or evocation
or adoration. In my ordinary life I face one brick
wall on one side and another brick wall on the
other. I do not even have words to distinguish
one brick wall from another and if there are
windows in yet another wall they give over to a
wall on the far side of any small opening. I envy
those who stand quietly on shores and watch
plovers. I do not know what a plover looks like
and I do not know if it makes a sound. The word
contains the word "lover," and also the word
"over" and that is yet another brick wall. I
believe in the power of birds, but I do not know,
not for a minute, how to describe their quivering
hearts or their flights or the mad plunge of
herons into salty marshes. A little while ago I
washed my face in clear water. I plunged right in,
my stupid eyes closed.

Glimmer

Before darkness, rumor, and after
darkness, rumor.

What do I know,
my hands outstretched and empty,

birds going hungry?

Large or Small

In a silence of my own making I
wait to hear the death shriek of
stars. Because they are so far away
I will wait for a long time. I don't
even look into the darkness dotted
with tiny lights. I turn over my
hand to see the lifeline etched in
my palm. Always a bad reader
of fortunes I have little to offer
in the way of threat or consolation.

Folly

I think tonight
that I am foolish
and afraid. No
one can say this
is untrue. I was
holding out
one hand a long
time and then
holding out
the other even
longer. A certain
vanity in this as I
have been told
often that I have
pretty hands. The
new polish turns
hard nails into
pearls.

Augury

Craters of ash,
lost nouns naming and
renaming themselves,
unwinding the black ribbon
around your lonely neck.
You had one finger to the wind.
You had shoes without laces.
You boiled away tea water
until the pot scorched
craters into unfathomable
ash. You stuck you hand
in it. You stuck your fist in,
you scooped something out.
Something hollowed out now,
and unfathomable.

A Family Story

My sister is enchanted by a homeless woman who paints birds.
Together they wander Central Park filling bird feeders,
leaving trails of crumbs. My father, who is also my sister's
father, spent the last years of his life almost homeless.
That is to say he lived like a homeless person in
an apartment in Paris. But as it turns out the apartment
in Paris was one room filled with old newspapers, broken
furniture, and food rotting on broken plates. You get
the picture. After he died my sister was the one to clean it up.
Now, when it gets cold or wet, the homeless woman who
paints birds moves into my sister's one room apartment.
The homeless artist hangs her paintings on my sister's
walls and pays for breakfast. She takes the dying cat
to the vet. The birds, lately mostly owls, look on.

Divination

1.

You must empty your head, willingly, to read the messages of
birds.

They will tell you, word by word.
What you need, what you already know.

2.

We were looking for an oracle
In the flight paths of birds
In their perfect formations

In their ceaseless wings,

3.

Something aggregates around
the birds.

their story, late and true.

They keep flying.

2.

We were looking for an oracle
In the flight paths of birds
In their perfect formations

In their ceaseless wings,

3.

Something aggregates around
    the birds.

    their story, late and true.

        They keep flying.

4.

The birds fly towards you
or they fly away

That makes all the difference.

5.

Consider now that the birds scrawl their messages and you are too far from the sky to read their words.

What then?

6.

On a dark line
    birds gather and part
    then return.

7.

How seeds held out
    in your hand
     are tokens.

In time
    the messengers will take
    everything you have.

8.

Look upward!

The birds in their long stretch.
Words in the sky.
When you look to the ground

drops of blood.

9.

Birds as oracles:

> Flying in perfect v formation birds
> change their position every five
> minutes

10.

Would the birds know?
    Would they tell me? Would I know
    To look up?

    If white birds, one way. If black, another.

11.

Two forms of augury
One of flight and one of feed

I am hungry. Give me to eat

12.

follow the birds they will lead you to honey

13.

Tonight the narrow moon beds
in clouds and otherwise it is dark and the birds
and all their messages have fled

Aloft

They say the fingers were much longer than the thumbs and curved ever so slightly. This, they say, meant that these creatures, early versions of us, used those curved fingers to climb trees. But of course, after that, the journey was all downwards and surely we know, don't we, though we never speak of it, that once we had beaks and claws. We had feathers and plumes. Once we were birds, and came flying out of the trees.

Respite

Tonight I would like, I swear, to get on my knees and kiss the
worn floorboards of the room in which I live. The boards glow
but don't shine. This reminds me, inexplicably, of a woman
I know, a photographer, who sat in a café in India. She was
there to take photos of the wounded and the lost. She had
taken many photos and was tired. She was, by then, an expert
at grief. Suddenly a flock of birds, swooped themselves out of
the sky and landed on the ground at her feet. No pictures came
of this moment. Astonishment only.

The Clairvoyant

We know what we do not know and when the belly, epitome of flesh, speaks through fissure, we take note. Thus birds, falling to earth, at once and without warning, signal a visible sign of angelic knowing. The birds cluster on earth, scratching dirt. Gather me, gather me to you, and I will give you bits of braided bread. I will hand out the seeds of mourning.

21 for 49

1. blood everywhere, this was said more than once
2. what we say when we say nothing
3. i am helpless in the face of
4. birds hover, they are not a symbol of
5. you could just touch the hand of one
6. it's still the same day, isn't it?
7. who is next to you, the one wearing a hat?
8. that one has stars on his shirt, that one has blood on his shirt
9. the noise goes on until you
10. plug up that hole with your bandana
11. cover your eyes, won't you, please?
12. why won't you cover your eyes?
13. you have only words
14. if white birds one way, if black another
15. in the dark it's impossible to know
16. the noise goes on
17. it's happening right now
18. we'll be right back, says no one
19. we're going to die, says someone
20. when you look to the ground, drops of blood
21. it's the same day and it goes on

Coda

In the evening that followed the terrible night friends and family gathered. The sun set, streaky and red-eyed, of course. The friends and family hugged one another and wept. They prepared to light candles. All this was to be expected. Pictures were taken. Birds flew above the assembled crowd. Of course there were photographs. Someone took photographs of the birds, flying in formation towards the west. All of this was to be expected under the circumstances. What was not expected was this: when the photos of birds were examined, when someone actually looked and counted, the number of birds, flying over the crowd that May evening, was exactly 49.